CONFESSIONS
OF A
DRAG QUEEN
TUPPERWARE® LADY

To: Josh

Keep it Fresh

♡

XOXO

Dee

Starring Kevin Farrell
as Dee W. Ieye

AND

with Nancy Sayles Kaneshiro

**Dee-Lightful
Publishing**
Powell, Ohio

Confessions of a Drag Queen Tupperware® Lady
by Kevin Farrell—as Dee W. Ieye
with Nancy Sayles Kaneshiro

Published by Dee-Lightful Publishing,
Powell, Ohio
c/o The Sayles Organization
22647 Ventura Blvd., #219, Woodland Hills, CA 91364
www.deewieye.com

Cover photo by David Arenas Photography; Interior and back cover caricature by Susanna Wong; Back cover photo (Kevin) by Ray Garcia; Back cover photo (Dee) by John Paschal

Editorial, Production Coordination, Publicity
The Sayles Organization, Woodland Hills, California
www.saylesorganization.com

Book and Cover design; production by Marion Redmond
Redmond and Associates, Los Angeles, California

Printed in the U.S.A.

Acknowledgments

The author would like to thank a few people who have led me to the major accomplishments in my life—including this one.

Geoff Laing for his never ending support and patience; Tom and Shirley Farrell—I could not have asked for more loving and encouraging parents; my brothers Mike and Matt. And Patricia Egelhoff—you are missed, but you helped a young man who didn't know he wanted to be an actor realize that spark—that hidden light—that needed to be explored and shared with the world.

Photographer John Paschal, who discovered that Dee has great legs and showed them to the world.

Glen Alen Gutierrez who created the "face" of Dee—thanks for being a great tutor! Kay, Dixie and Auntie B—they say to be the best, you must learn from the best. Thanks for sharing your considerable talents.

Nancy Kaneshiro for approaching me at that party and saying my story must be told.

Special thanks to Tupperware for allowing me to take their wonderful products into people's homes, make people laugh and fill my creative heart.

And for the countless hostesses and customers I've met over the years. You have provided me with a platform to perform, and for that I am forever grateful.

The Beginning...
A Curtsy
To The Queens

Before I tell my story, I must give credit where credit is due. It was never MY idea to dress in drag and sell Tupperware.

The first drag queen Tupperware Lady, to my knowledge, was Jeff Sumner in Los Angeles. He played Pam Teflon back in 1995 and sold till 2003. A very, very funny guy who got a lot of press at the time. (I Googled him. I was amazed!)

Then came Kay Sedia (Oscar Quintero) and Dixie Longate (Kris Andersson). They both joined in 2001 and started selling as their characters. They were quick to take off and are still selling today and doing very well.

All three of these gentlemen helped pave my way to become the success that I am. I really have to give them credit, especially to Oscar, because he was the one who approached me in 2005 to sell as Dee W. Ieye.

And now, following in our high-heeled footsteps, we have Aunt Barbara in Long Island, Anita Longhorn in San Diego, Aunt Lola Cabana in Chicago, as well as Ana Robix, Misty O. Tupperware and Aunt Cassie Rolle in Los Angeles, to name a few. Very talented men who have taken their talents, put on a wig and gone into Tupperware sales to make the parties fun and exciting.

My wig is off to them—for we are all different in our own respective roles. Congratulations, "ladies!" I love you and I continue to be inspired and challenged by you. You make me a better person. Thank you.

Kevin

Table of Contents

CHAPTER I

Kevin Farrell,
Boy Actor
or
Hooray for Hollywood

I moved to Los Angeles in 1996 as an actor after I was cast on an episode of *Frasier*. (I played the look-alike of Frasier's brother, Niles, and thanks to cable syndication, I still get stopped on the street!) I decided to move from Chicago and come out to LA and see where my acting career would take me. I worked in television—mostly in sitcoms—on and off for the first six or seven years. I worked a lot, but never really made enough money to sustain myself, so I was always trying to make ends meet by doing the usual stuff—waiting tables and working catered parties just to pay the bills.

In 2004, I was involved in an event called the Best in Drag Show, a fund-raiser for an organization called Aid for AIDS in Los Angeles, where they raised money for people who are living with HIV and AIDS. It's a one-night fund-raiser where seven or eight drag queen contestants actually pose as beauty queens from any state they want to be from. I chose Tennessee and my character's name was Dee W. Ieye. Her back-story was that she was the sole heir to the Jack Daniels fortune but, to her family's dismay, she had a drinking problem. She would get about thirty days of sobriety, but then they would have a tasting at the distillery and she'd fall off the wagon and have to start all over again. So I played that character in 2004, I did the fund-raiser, helped to raise a lot of money and swore I would never dress in drag again. Dee was going back into the closet, so to speak.

About the same time, Oscar, a friend of mine, was selling Tupperware, in drag, and he'd been doing it for about three years, making some pretty good money at it, too. So when he saw me play that character, Dee W. Ieye, he said, "You should go sell Tupperware in drag!" And I told him, "And you should go f-yourself!" because I was just not going to do that. "You're really funny, it works for you," I told him, "but I'm not going to do it." Well, he must have asked me at least half a dozen more times and I finally said yes...just to shut him up!

At that time you could join Tupperware for, like, thirty bucks, so I did it! I got my "kit" but I had no idea what

I was doing or where I was going to do it. I did my first party with my friend and there were three people there. I think I sold about $107 worth of Tupperware. It was a total disaster and I thought *well, maybe this isn't for me.* But…I didn't give up! I kept trying to get family and friends to have parties and then started branching out to their friends and neighbors who would have a party. It was about a year-and-a-half before my business really took off, before I actually started to do more than just one party a month and actually started to see a little bit of income coming from it, so I still kept working other places part time.

Two years into the business, I began to see that I was working more, booking more parties, selling more Tupperware, and it just started to take off. People started to book more parties, and friends of friends of friends started asking about me. I was working more and more and selling more and more and before long, I was being recognized in the company for my sales. For four years running, I was Tupperware's number one salesperson in North America. Of everyone who sold Tupperware in Canada and the US, I was the number one personal seller. That was me selling over $230,000 per year!

So that's how I got started, and being an actor really helped me because I know how to command the stage, command a room, project my voice and I have been blessed with good comic timing. I enjoy being on the stage and making people laugh. So once I designed this character around the whole Tupperware thing, it really became a way for me to perform and entertain people, and not be counting on the entertainment business to employ me. All of a sudden, I didn't have to be on the

TV shows, I didn't have to go the auditions at 4 o'clock on a Friday afternoon at Paramount Studios in traffic, I was able to control my income, and control how much I wanted to work and if I didn't want to work. For the first time, I was in the driver's seat of my career and my income. I didn't have to count on someone else for my livelihood. So many actors are in the situation where they are competing against so many other people for one job. I found myself not having to do that anymore and I really felt like I didn't need to be boy actor anymore.

While I did a ton of television appearances, I was never a regular on a TV show so I was never afforded the opportunity to get comfortable in that arena of being in front of a camera. It would always be me coming in and working a couple of days and being with a bunch of people who didn't know me but were already comfortable in their roles and with each other. I felt the pressure was so great for me to be perfect every time and to not screw up, because time is money on the set of a television show, plus I had to try to fit into an already established group of actors…it was totally nerve-wracking.

I got my training in college and while living in Chicago for ten years, working in plays, live in front of an audience, and I just felt that was my niche, that's where I was most comfortable. And now, I don't have to be perfect every night doing the Tupperware show, and it's always different every night. I have the basic structure, I know the products I want to talk about, but something out of the ordinary *always* happens. A woman's cell phone goes off at an inopportune moment, or someone walks in late, right on my punchline, and I have to roll with the punches. As a good performer, I have to react and play off the situation, so it's not unlike doing a set of improv every night. Just like with any live performance, I might get a heckler I have to deal with, obnoxious, drunken women or girls who just talk too much sitting in the front row, and I have to work around those things, stay in character and do my show. And there have been times, I can tell you, where I've wanted to drop the character and tell someone off, because *hey, I'm performing!* If you don't want to pay attention, fine…but go outside and take your conversation somewhere else. *Quit yackin' in the front row and keepin' everybody else from having a good time!* I never want to break character or have the whole room turn on me, because that can get ugly. That happened once and let me tell you, it wasn't pretty. But that's the joy of live performance.

So with the television thing, once it became harder and harder for me to get cast because of the sheer number of actors going for the same roles in L.A., I was going out for tiny roles on sitcoms and found myself up against major players, major actors with big names, and I thought, *really? They're going to do this little teeny role on this show?* It seems like the entertainment field had shifted once reality television began to take over and people who were on a sitcom a few years ago but you hadn't seen in a while started taking the roles that guys like me would have been right for, but because they were a household name, everyone got pushed down a rung on the ladder. It seemed like a losing battle and I didn't want to play the game anymore. I didn't want to do one line on *Hannah Montana* just because it was a job. I was having more fun at my parties with twenty-five women, with me dancing around and playing this crazy character, Dee W. Ieye, and coming home with a bag full of money. It seemed like a no-brainer to me.

It's not that I wouldn't like to work as an actor as Kevin again. I always told myself that once I hit fifty or sixty, I'd probably work all the time, especially commercially, because I'm a character actor, but it got to the point in LA that I couldn't wait that long! Even though sixty is usually considered dead by Hollywood standards, somebody has to do those Prilosec commercials, and I'd be a shoo-in! I'm funny and I'm quirky and I should be booking commercials right and left, but I just don't have time to grow into my looks!

It was hard for me. I wanted to know what the universe was trying to tell me...I'm a big communicator with the universe. If I'm so talented, and I was brought to Hollywood for whatever reason, why am I not booking commercials? I was working in television a lot, but not getting the commercials I was going up for, so maybe I'm not supposed to be a commercial actor, maybe I'm supposed to be in TV. And once that began to dry up, I felt that I really need to be performing, because I really believe that whatever you're meant to do on this planet—and this is very Oprah-ish, I know—but something happens inside of me when I'm playing this character, and I'm in the groove with the room, and everyone's laughing and having a good time, I know I'm supposed to be doing that. Am I supposed to be an entertainer in drag only, and not as Kevin, the actor? I don't know. Kevin the stage actor worked a lot in Chicago, so I found myself asking those questions that there are really no answers to, but I felt

I was doing something that I was supposed to do. So is playing Dee W. Ieye my higher purpose? I don't know, but what I find is that she is so likable and people just love to be around her—men and women alike. I do parties for straight men, and they have a blast—as long as they're not close-minded about what I do, because there's a stigma about drag from people who are not educated about the different levels of drag. There are people who dress up who try to look like women and fool you, and that's certainly not me. All you have to do is look at my picture and you'll see that I'm a clown, an actor who plays a character, not unlike Flip Wilson who played Geraldine. I was young when that show was on the air, and my parents loved Geraldine, but everyone knew that he was a man in drag. And Milton Berle in the early fifties? That was classic!

I'm not one of those guys who goes to clubs and lip-syncs to Madonna songs, I really believe that when I put that wig on and those heels, I'm Dee W. Ieye. I'm her…she's a real person. When my partner Geoff and I go shopping, he'll ask, "Does Dee need anything today?" Or, "maybe Dee would look good in that!" So we think of her as a person, which is a lot healthier than saying "me" in those situations! Some days, I'll tell you, it can be so confusing!

CHAPTER 2

Ancient History, BD (Before Dee)!

After moving to Los Angeles in 1996 to shoot that episode of *Frasier*, I worked a lot in television but it still was very spotty. I probably did fifteen or twenty television appearances on shows, including *Veronica's Closet, Malcolm in the Middle, The Hughleys, Working, Conrad Bloom, Friends, General Hospital, One Life to Live, The Young and the Restless, Ally McBeal* and *Boston Legal.* I worked a lot on the David E. Kelley shows because he seemed to like me. And the people who used to cast for *Dharma and Greg*, Nikki Valko and Ken Miller, had me on their favorites list and brought me in for everything they cast. They would always see me for everything that I was right for. I didn't always get it, of course, but it's nice to be called when they say *OK, let's bring in the top five character actors in Los Angeles.* I was playing with the big guys, and that worked well for a really long time.

At the same time, I worked for a number of other companies, one of which was the Da Camera Society, a chamber music and historical society that works out of Mount St. Mary's College. What they did was to stage classical music quartet concerts in historical sites in Los Angeles, so it was really fascinating. For example, if it were a Frank Lloyd Wright home, we would do a concert in the living room. Other venues included the Bradbury Building in downtown Los Angeles and historic churches all over Pasadena. You could actually sit in these really cool historic places and listen to this fantastic classical music. So I did that for two or three years, working in their ticket office. While I loved the music, I felt as though creatively I was being wasted.

I had so much experience being a stage actor in Chicago that I just really wanted to perform, so before Tupperware I was just doing all these odds and ends. I would go on auditions during the day but if I didn't get the job, then I would be back catering or at the concert music place. The job that I held for two years before I broke into Tupperware, perhaps the most satisfying job I've ever had, was working at a foster home for troubled children called Hollygrove. Hollygrove was on Vine Street, just north of Melrose and it actually was where Marilyn Monroe lived for a while.

It's a live-in facility where the kids do not have the

option to leave. They have been taken away from their parents because of abuse by the parents to them, or by them to the parents. A lot of the kids were a danger to their parents, threatening them with guns and knives, so they had to be taken away, whether it was from their own homes or foster homes. So they would come to this facility where they lived with us 24/7. I was a child care counselor and I basically walked these kids through a daily routine. My shift was Sunday through Wednesday, from 11am to 11pm, so I did twelve-hour days with these kids. It made me appreciate my upbringing and my family so much more, working with these kids, because they came from some real rough stuff. And these kids were damaged. Sexual abuse and verbal abuse just made these kids really mean and hateful. They would swing at us and bite us, so we had to be trained to restrain them from hurting themselves or any adults. The age range was five to twelve years old. We're not talking teenagers, these are little kids. The youngest I ever worked with was five, and that poor little kid had seen some bad, bad stuff at his house. Most of the kids had dealt with so many abandonment issues, they thought they were all so unlovable.

It was a facility where we tried to teach them values. We taught them caring and friendship and a list of seven or eight values, and we worked with them 24/7. There were adults with them all the time. The kids who were old enough to go to school and safe enough to leave campus went across the street to Vine Street Elementary School. They walked to and from, but always with adults. These kids were never out of an adult's view, ever. And when they were asleep, there was always an adult in the hallway in a chair who could see the bedrooms at all times, because these kids were hopping into bed with each other, even at their ages. They had to have adult supervision at all times.

One thing we learned was never to allow ourselves to be alone with a child, because that was bad news. They could call abuse on counselors and we would automatically be fired, because the courts always had to rule for the children. So the kids could lie through their teeth, and often did. If I was alone in a room with a kid and he said *Mr. Kevin touched me,* I was done, whether or not it was true. So there had to be two adults in the room with children at all times. I did that for two years.

They taught us as child care counselors that we had to leave our work at work, but it was so hard to come home at night and just dust off that day, because there were days when it was just really hard emotionally to watch what these kids went through. It was about that time when I got introduced to Tupperware. I was doing Tupperware parties at the same time I was still at Hollygrove, and I remember sitting around laughing with the other counselors about the fact I was selling Tupperware in drag. They all thought that was just hysterical.

After I left counseling, I still catered on and off while I made the transition from Tupperware as a part time thing to full time. It was about a year-and-a-half before I saw it was something financially that I could do without having to have another job to make ends meet.

So as a struggling actor trying not to be a starving actor, I worked for several catering companies, including Good Gracious Catering and It's Our Party Catering. They would always drop me in whenever they had events like weddings or bar mitzvahs. There was a lady who lived in a beautiful condo in Beverly Glen, and I always did her Passover dinner for her. One night we showed up and the caterer had forgotten to pack the matzah, so someone had to do a run to a local market. It was, like, *Oh My God! We have no matzah!* It was really fun for me, since I had never celebrated Passover before, but everybody was really cranky because the service was long and nobody had eaten. And we're trying to put all the food together in the kitchen, as the caterer, and while the kitchen should have been off-limits, the guests kept coming into the kitchen and getting in the way, because they were hungry! Those were fun times.

14

CHAPTER 3

Dee...
A Star is Born!

I've always had this vision about what my life was going to be like. I really believe that you manifest into your life what you envision and I'm into the whole *Secret* thing, cutting pictures out of magazines and creating a storyboard for your life, and that's how you make it happen. It started for me in the seventh grade when I did my first play and got hooked by being on stage and being a performer. Then I went to high school and was involved in the drama club, and did more plays, including my first musical—Mom and Dad didn't even know I could sing—and I got the lead in "Godspell" in my sophomore year. That just led me into the musical theater world and I went away to college at Miami University of Ohio and did theater there. I then went to Actors Theater in Louisville and worked there as an actor for nine months before moving to Chicago, where I was part of a theater company for ten years. Tons of theater. I always knew that was what I wanted to do. I felt most comfortable on stage, I felt like that was my home. When the lights went down and I was on stage and the audience was looking up at me, I felt like that was where I needed to be. I am in sync with the universe when I am onstage. So I always wanted to be an actor, but it wasn't like I necessarily needed to be a famous actor. I just wanted to be a performer who got paid to do what he did. I didn't want to need a survival job, like so many actors do, waiting tables, catering parties, working temp jobs, but I did all of that stuff. All during the ten years I lived in Chicago, I worked in the mail room of insurance brokerage firms, I waited tables, I did it all...always had a day job so that I could do what I wanted to do at night. I feel like I still want to do that. I'm an actor and I want to be a paid entertainer. That's what I always wanted in my life. So when I moved to California and started doing television work, I thought *OK, one step closer, now I'm in the big leagues, now I'm in television.* I sort of left theater behind, and while I wasn't making a lot of money, I was getting paid to be on television shows, and I thought this is it! But it wasn't enough to live on so I was still waiting tables, working in catering, doing odd jobs to be able to pay my bills.

Then the Tupperware thing came along. It wasn't successful at first but what happened was that I was able to perform, I was able to make people laugh, and all of a sudden, I realized that I had manifested in my world what I had always wanted. I wanted to be a paid entertainer... well now I'm a paid entertainer through Tupperware. It just came in a totally different package, and that's what I tell people now, whenever I speak or do training. You may think your life is this picture, and while you might get what you want, sometimes it's in a different box with different wrapping paper. That's what happened to me. I got to be a paid entertainer, which is what I am. I do this full time, I sell Tupperware in drag. It's my full-time job. While it's not on television, I'm still kind of onstage but now it's a different picture. I love that story because you never really know what's going to be handed to you.

When I had been approached several times by Oscar to sell Tupperware, I told him *no, I don't want to do that.* I didn't want to dress up like a woman and sell Tupperware because that's what he was doing. I kept saying no, but the lesson in that is that you never really know what you're saying no to. If I would have continued to say no to him and not taken this opportunity—well—this has entirely changed my life. I'm able to pay all my bills because of this character I play, I've built a house based on the money made by playing this character, and what's nice, too, is that this character has been able to branch out beyond Tupperware. I emcee events, I show up for corporate parties or private parties, so she (Dee) has really stepped out from behind the Tupperware logo and become her own entity, her own performer, her own brand. And now I have people in Hollywood chasing me because it's a story they want to produce or put on television and that's fascinating to me. This is what I've always wanted, but I thought it was going to be about Kevin, the boy actor, and what it turned out to be is Kevin the salesman, Kevin the businessman, and Dee, the drag queen persona.

I can say honestly I've never sold Tupperware in long pants. Now, if I recruit someone new, it's my obligation to go to her first show, and I will go as Kevin. I would never go as Dee because she would steal the show, and that wouldn't be fair. I would never have imagined myself where I am in my life. I certainly didn't move to California to be a drag queen, it's just taken on a whole life of its own, which is really amazing.

CHAPTER 4

Dee's OUT!

My father is retired military. Colonel. Army. National Guard. I wouldn't say it's a conservative family, but a typical Midwestern Ohio family. So I had been selling Tupperware for a year-and-a-half or two years and they knew I was becoming very successful. I was doing really well, I was selling a lot of product. I think that by my second year, I was number five in the nation, so it didn't take me very long to start climbing the ranks in sales. My parents were very proud of me, but I wasn't telling them how I was selling. When I first started selling, I had two different business cards made up. I had one with Dee W. Ieye's picture on it in full Technicolor, and then I had a plain, black-and-white business card with Kevin Farrell's name on it, the Tupperware logo and my phone number, so that was my business card for every day. If you were having a Tupperware party with Dee, however, you would get the one with her photo on it.

Now, I have two older brothers. There are seven years between me and my next oldest brother. I sent the card with Dee W. Ieye's picture on it to my oldest brother Michael and I said, "This is how I sell Tupperware" and he was floored. He said NO WAY, and I said, "Michael, this is why I'm so successful. It's because of this character I'm playing. I'm not just selling Tupperware, I'm selling Tupperware as this character." He said, "Wow, that's amazing!" I asked, "Do you think we should tell Mom and Dad?" And he said, "You know what? I don't THINK so!" Fine, we agreed, we're not going to tell Mom and Dad that I dress up in drag to sell Tupperware.

I call my parents every Saturday morning without fail. I picked up the phone one Saturday morning after having this conversation with Michael. My parents are on two extensions, as they are every Saturday, and I hear my mother say, "I saw your business card!" And I just froze, because I didn't know which she had seen. "Really?" I asked. She said, "Yes." "Is it the one with the picture on it?" I asked nervously? "Yes!" she said, and I knew the jig was up. My brother had shown my parents the business card with Dee W. Ieye's picture on it and I thought it would be downhill from there, but it wasn't. My parents were laughing! They were actually laughing on the phone. Even my father, my retired colonel, military father, was just tickled! That just made me so happy because I wasn't exactly sure how they were going to take it, but it made me realize that my family is much more open-minded than I might have given them credit for. It all came back to conversations I'd had with them before about Flip Wilson who played the character Geraldine on his show, Milton Berle dressed up in drag way back in the early days of television, and Dustin Hoffman playing Tootsie. Hoffman's character couldn't get hired as an actor, and I couldn't get hired as much as I wanted to as an actor, so I started playing this character in drag. I think that helped my parents in accepting the fact that I was just an actor playing a role to sell Tupperware. And the more I sold and the more successful I became in the Tupperware business, my father just became more and more proud of me.

I was on a Columbus morning show one spring when I went home, as Dee, as a local celebrity…and as Kevin. They interviewed me first as Dee, then during a break, I ran and took my makeup off and returned as Kevin, and they interviewed me as Kevin about the business. So you saw the nation's number one Tupperware lady moments ago and now you get to meet the real person, and there I was. It was great because people could see the difference between that crazy blond balloon clown, as I call her, and Kevin, the businessman, the smart guy underneath the makeup.

The next time I went home, I went on the morning show again, but only as Dee W. Ieye. The reason I'm telling this story is that when I came home after that appearance and I was up in my bedroom at my parents' house, my father came down the hallway and said, "I have to tell you something. I know that I don't say this very often and I know that your mother tells you more often how much she loves you, but I have to tell you that I'm so proud of you and what you've done in your business and that your mother and I love you very much." He started to get choked up a little and I was just a wreck because with my father's history in the military, there's that stoic attitude that prevails. I think I've seen him cry twice in my entire life. And that meant so much to me for my father to say how proud he was for me to be doing what I do, which is just insane. Soon after, I made the decision to move back to Columbus to be near to my family, to be closer to home as I grow older. It's great that I can take my business back with me because there is such a demand for me to do what I do in Ohio, and I'm so grateful because with so many businesses you just couldn't do that. If I worked for an employer in California, I couldn't just uproot myself and move myself back to Ohio, so with this, I can move my business wherever I want to. I'm very grateful that my family is so supportive.

My other brother, Matthew, is a retired police officer. He works for a special anti-terrorism task force and he's seen my show, as my other brother has. They're just tickled, though I don't think they'd parade me around to all their friends, but my oldest brother has been in the entertainment business as a musician for years and understands the whole entertainment thing. He went with me to my second appearance on "Good Morning Columbus" and he was just a proud older brother watching his little brother on the morning news as a celebrity Tupperware lady.

CHAPTER 5

Diving Head First into Tupperware

I like working with food. I'm a good cook. I love to cook. My partner Geoff and I are both good cooks. We cook for too many people, though. Even when it's just the two of us, we make enough for fifty people, so it seemed almost natural that I work for a company that had to do with food, and food storage and food prep. I've been approached by other companies to come and work for them in the beauty business or the jewelry business or the clothes business or whatever, because they know how good I am in sales, and I'm just not interested. First of all, I can't because I'm a director in Tupperware, and

I signed an agreement which precludes my working for another direct-selling company, so I legally can't work for anyone else. I can't sell sheets, I can't sell jewelry, so this is my company and it's the company I want to be with. I believe in their product, I believe in them as a company as a whole, and I especially believe in the fact that it's a company that's based on empowering women.

I love the history of Tupperware because back in the day, it was the first time that women were able to get out of the house. They became Tupperware ladies, and that was unheard of in a time when women stayed home. They were housewives, and now all of a sudden they were becoming their own bosses, they got out of the house and no longer lived in a house where only the husband was the breadwinner. It was empowering to give women the opportunity to spread their wings and that's still true today.

I meet a lot of women who are finding empowerment in owning their own businesses because they always sort of lived under the radar of the husband who was the breadwinner and whose permission was needed about any expenditure of money. Now these women are out there doing their own thing and for some women, it's actually even giving them the power to walk away from relationships that are unhealthy or even abusive. I hear about those stories all the time at our annual Jubilee conventions. These women get up and tell their stories. It's sad but it's inspiring at the same time because Tupperware gave them the voice to be able to get up and walk away from those men, because they could start providing for themselves and their children and didn't have to depend on staying in an abusive relationship.

I love those stories. There was a story that Geoff and I heard one year of a Hispanic girl who worked at a supermarket and she was always out in the parking lot in the rain and the crappy weather collecting the carts. Her husband and kids would come to pick her up but she didn't want her kids seeing their mother pushing shopping carts in the rain. She didn't want to be that mother. She didn't want to be identified like that to her kids. So she started her own Tupperware business, became really successful and completely changed her family's life. I love those kinds of stories.

Another girl came from a meager background and stepped out of it through Tupperware. She moved up in the company and became this enormous seller with a huge *downline*. She recruited her whole neighborhood who had a huge circle of family and friends. They all worked really, really hard. They didn't wait for the business to come to them, they went out and found the business. This particular girl was cleaning people's houses, and she said , "I don't want to clean other people's houses, I want somebody to clean my house!" And now, she and her husband have built this huge empire in Chicago. They're millionaires. So that's my goal, for Geoff and me to build another huge empire in Tupperware in Ohio, reaching out to help others achieve their dreams and be financially independent.

I have to realize that my strength is selling as Dee W. Ieye, it's not *recruiting* as Dee W. Ieye, and that's why I'm now starting an enterprise called Kevin's Kitchen in Ohio. I can come to your house as Kevin, the man behind the makeup, and work with just a handful of women. I can teach you how to make pasta, I can show you how to make salsa or a cake in the microwave, but I'm also going to be able to share with you the opportunities that Tupperware has as Kevin talking to you and not Dee, because Dee's just this big blond crazy drag queen from Tennessee. It's hard to take her seriously.

My heart can come out as I talk to you as Kevin and I can tell you how this company can change your life like it's changed mine—the guy who found a way to make a great living. I think I can still sell as much and train as much as Kevin as I do as Dee. So I'm looking forward to using Kevin as the recruiter, because hey, I can be as much fun as Dee! Growing my team, that's my future in Tupperware. I have to think about the life expectancy of Dee W. Ieye. How much longer do I want to play that character and schlep out of the house with all that stuff, because that gets to be draining five nights a week. How can I build my future and how can I build my retirement, because my retirement is based on my having a huge downline that I can continue to grow and train and mentor. Then those girls are going to go off and they're going to make a lot of money and develop their own companies and become their own entrepreneurs, and that little percentage that I see from those girls floats to the top, a little percentage of many adds up to a huge amount of money (which, by the way, is how that couple in Chicago became millionaires, because a little percentage of thousands comes to the surface).

Otherwise, I don't know what to do about retirement. I'm not the normal run-of-the-mill guy who worked for a company for thirty-five years or a career military man like my father. That's not my path, so I have to find out how I'm going to take care of myself when I retire as a direct seller for a company. Healthcare—all of that—it's a lot to think about. I never quite made enough as an actor to qualify for benefits through the unions, so it was like being trapped between a rock and a hard place, when all I really ever wanted to do was to be a paid performer, not be famous, just not have to hold down an outside job to pay my bills. I wanted to be able to pay my bills, buy a house, buy a car and do all that stuff through my skills as an actor and it's come to me through Dee W. Ieye.

I heard the story of a girl who worked as a housekeeper through her entire career as an actress, and she became a familiar face in sitcoms. She said cleaning houses gave her the flexibility to go on auditions and pursue acting without getting a regular "day job." I had to laugh when I heard that she left a note for one of her clients after cleaning her apartment. "You're out of Windex," the note said, "and my Mr. Belvedere airs tonight."

I've tried to tell other performers that Tupperware provides the opportunity to perform while you're pursuing an acting career. If you don't want to find a character, and if you're good at standup, do a standup routine around the selling of Tupperware. You don't have to be a drag queen, you could be Larry the Cable Guy, you could be Kathy Griffin, you could be Rita Rudner—any of those people who are really good in front of an audience—and just spin your story around the selling of Tupperware. Then you have the flexibility to go on auditions.

My problem was that I got so popular doing Tupperware, it actually interfered with my being an actor in Los Angeles.

The tables turned in such a way that if I had to be in South Orange County for a Tupperware party on Wednesday at 5pm, I'd have to leave LA no later than 2, but if I had a callback from Paramount or Sony, I couldn't go on that callback. So in a way, I was being untrue to my agent, because my agent was doing his job to get me out on the calls, but then I was unable to follow through on the jobs. I am a man of integrity and that was making me feel really bad, so I had to get to a point where I thought *this ain't workin'.* If you booked a Tupperware party with me four months ago, my obligation was to show up to your house because you are going to make sure that thirty-five people are there for me on Wednesday at 5 o'clock. I could not find it in myself to call you and say I'm not coming to your party, cancel it, call everybody and tell them not to come because I have a callback at Paramount, and I don't even know if I'm going to get that job. This was a sure thing for me. I knew that I could drive to Orange County, perform and sell.

Most actors who have regular day jobs can always call in a sub to cover their shift, but who am I going to call to do what I do? Now, regular Tupperware salespeople can cover for one another in a pinch, if there's an emergency with a kid or an illness. These girls cover for each other all the time. Who am I going to call? They're coming to see me! My friend, Dixie Longate, had overbooked his parties and called me in to cover one night. But it put additional pressure on me because THEY wanted Dixie and now they were getting Dee! No matter how good I was as Dee, I wasn't Dixie. But you know what, the hostess told me afterward that she was a little nervous, but that she and her friends totally enjoyed me. And that's why I can't just send any numb-nuts in to cover for me, because he (she?) would be representing me, even though I would feel comfortable sending in Dixie or Kay Sedia or Aunt Barbara. But if you were some guy who was new to Tupperware and trying to sell in drag, I wouldn't send you because you would be representing me and my company.

CHAPTER 6

Kevin
vs.
Dee

Every year there's a big Tupperware Jubilee when the entire Tupperware sales force from all over the United States and Canada comes together and we do recognition and training, and it's basically our big conference for the year. In 2005, the first year I attended the conference, I dressed as Dee on one of the nights—it was called Fun Night—so it seemed appropriate. I attended the conference as Kevin, but I showed up on Fun Night as Dee W. Ieye. So THAT was a fun night! But over the next few years, I found it really wasn't appropriate for me to dress up in drag when we were all gathered together as a sales force, because I know that I'm not everyone's cup of tea. I know that there are people in Tupperware who have misgivings about how I do my show and how I dress up. Even though Tupperware embraces it and corporate won't say, "you can't do that," it's a fine line I walk.

So after going to the convention that first year and dressing up, and once I started to get a name for myself—Kevin Farrell, that huge, huge seller—I wanted to be recognized as Kevin. Dee is a *character* and I step out of myself to play that character. When I am that character, I am not Kevin, so it was important that Kevin show up to the conventions and that Kevin, not that character, relate and introduce himself to the other sales people, so I stopped dressing. I just thought that it's not the time or the place. I thought, *just let people get to know Kevin*. However, for the last few years, I *have* dressed, but only on Fun Night, a night when we're free to do whatever we want. I do it because there are people who do want to see me, there are people in that sales force who love Dee W. Ieye and don't get a chance to see her except on YouTube and Facebook. I don't want to fail to celebrate her as a character because a lot of people get a lot of joy in meeting her and talking with her and having their pictures taken with her, but it wasn't right to show up that way in a serious business meeting context, when we're all together as a sales force . Plus, since there are people there who really don't want to see a guy dressed in drag, I don't want to rub their faces in it. I'll be available for people who want to see me (as Dee) on our own time.

The education and training development department

has contacted me on several occasions to come to the national conferences and train on product and train on my sales technique—my sales technique as *Kevin*, the salesperson, not as Dee, the drag queen. There's a big difference between those two entities. So when I go as Kevin to talk about the product and the parties and the promotion, it's all Kevin, because Kevin is the smart businessman behind the fun character who is Dee W. Ieye.

While there are a lot of people who know that I dress in drag to sell Tupperware, there are even more people who know me as Kevin Farrell, the successful seller, but have no idea it's Kevin Farrell who dresses in drag. I still have girls come up to me and say, "How in the world did you sell $31,000 worth of Tupperware in one month?" And that's when I say, "Well, I do a show." And if they continue to ask questions, then I will show them my business card, with Dee's picture on it! Most Tupperware girls will say, "I can't ask a hostess to have thirty-five people at her party." The party average, and the business module that Tupperware uses to train its people, is six to seven people, maybe more, but it's generally between six and ten people. And the sales that are generated from a party that size average $450. That is how Tupperware rates success in its business module: three parties per week, $450 per party. Now, everyone goes all over the map with that, but for me, my minimum party is $1200. I feel that with what I go through, with the entertainment and the wig and the lashes and doing my show, I feel it's not worth my time unless we sell $1000 worth of product at a party. So I created my own business module to say a minimum thirty to thirty-five people and we're going to sell a minimum $1500 in product....and we usually do. Even now, with the economy what it is, we can get to that $1500 with thirty eager buyers. It's hard to get to that level with ten or twelve people in the room. These days, it's nearly impossible. So that's why I pat myself on the back for becoming a smart businessman, for figuring out how to beat the economy. We have all these cards stacked against us right now because of the state of our economy. With so many people out of work, how do we come out from under that? How can we still be successful?

During the recession, I was selling more than I have ever sold in my career and people were asking, "How does he DO that? He's got to be smart!" And that's why I want to train people now, in or out of a wig, so I can find those people I can help. I want to find those women whose husbands have lost their jobs, who have kids in dance class and they've got to find that extra money to put them in tights. That extra money comes from selling Tupperware. They don't have to do what I do, in fact, I don't WANT them to do what I do. I tell them this: I want you to do what you know how to do best and if there are four pieces of Tupperware that you love and you use in your home and you're passionate about, those are the pieces of Tupperware that I'm going to help you go out to do parties with. Have six or seven people at your girlfriend Susie's house on a Wednesday night and you're going to sell $450 and go home with $100 in your pocket.

I have been so successful in this business that I'm at a point where I want to help other people be successful. It's hard for me to find these people when I'm in a wig, because as Dee, I'm this larger-than-life character. As

Kevin, however, I can tell you how passionate I am about my business and I can be frank with you, but it's hard for me to tell you how much Tupperware has changed my life with that wig on my head. So if I want to be sincere, I can't really do it as Dee. It just doesn't translate. That's why people are always asking me, "Why aren't you recruiting more?" Well, when I'm Dee, I can be in front of you as the character, but I can't talk seriously about business until I've "hung her up" for the night. So I'm always looking for those girls I can have serious conversations with, someone I can sit down with and talk about how Tupperware has changed my life. But I have to do it as Kevin; it's difficult to do it as Dee. Now that I'm in Ohio, I'm actually finding those individuals. I'm growing my team and I think it's just awesome helping others become successful in their own businesses as I have in mine.

CHAPTER 7

The Business of Acting

I didn't study business in college, I studied how to be an actor—how to stand on stage, how to project, how to do all the things that well-trained stage actors are really good at. I never thought that training would be so helpful in selling, but it absolutely is. I've been able to develop that entertaining character but also become a good businessman, even thought I didn't study business. I know good customer service, because I appreciate it when I go into a store, so I give that back to my customers. I know my product, I know the featured benefits of my Tupperware, which helps to sell. If you sit in on one of my shows, I talk about why a certain item is better in your kitchen than anything else. What does it do for you? Does it have more uses than what I'm buying it for? Can I get more use of it than just its intended purpose? If you don't know your product, if you don't know why it's good, then you can't sell it! I also feel that you have to be passionate about what you're selling, no matter what it is. When I'm doing live Tupperware demonstrations, when I'm showing a product and I'm passionate about it, it spreads through the room. You may not want it, you may not feel you need it, but if I feel passionate about it, and about what I'm doing as a business person, it just helps me to be that much more successful. I don't know if I could be as successful selling something else, because I love Tupperware. I use it in my house, in my cabinets, in my fridge.

I'm asked if it gets old, if I have to drag myself (pardon the pun) to these parties. The answer is yes, it does. If I'm doing five parties a week, it's a full-time job...it's all I do. And when I'm not selling, I'm doing the administrative work that goes with the parties. A lot of follow-up work. If something doesn't show up in an order, or the wrong product shows up, I have to handle it. And since Tupperware offers a lifetime guarantee on its products, if you have something at your house that you bought forty years ago and it cracked, and you bring it to a party, I have to replace that product. It's all part of my job as a person who works for Tupperware. I take my job very seriously and I think that's why I'm successful. That's how I make my livelihood. That's how I pay my bills. That's how I built a house. So it does get old every so often and I have to sort of reinvent myself, but sometimes that's just changing an outfit. Now it's not just changing my hair, because I like my signature hair, but it's just doing things differently… like writing new material for every sales special, new jokes, so that keeps my show from getting stale. I treat this like a standup show that evolves all the time. Sometimes it'll come in the middle of a show and I'll think, "oh, I've got to keep that in the act" or someone at a party will give me an idea or blurt something out that I wind up adding to my show.

What doesn't get old is the time Dee spends when she's "on." It's always a new group of girls, a new chemistry in the room, and that keeps it fresh. Of course, I never get tired of the laughs! But it is tiring. I work really hard, but when I'm off, I enjoy not being in drag and spending time with family and friends, traveling and enjoying life. I love her. I love Dee W. Ieye, and I think what's successful about her is that she's likable. I've tried to figure out why people like her, why they like to be around her and I think it's a reflection of who Kevin is (me) and I'm happy that people want to be around me! I think there's a lot of me in Dee and I'm not mean and hateful, and I don't have the kind of mouth Dee has. I remember when my mother saw my show with my military father, and she had a good time but said, "I wish you didn't have to cuss so much!" And while Dee talks like a truck driver, I never want to offend anyone, it's not my intent. Kevin wouldn't do that…and neither would Dee.

My show isn't for everyone. If you would prefer not to listen to a bit of a bawdy show, I completely understand. I've had women old and young who come up and say, "I've never had such fun at a Tupperware party." I especially love it when it comes from eighty-year-old women who've seen it all!

What really touches me is when people come up to me and tell me they're going through a really hard time, their sister has cancer, their best friend died last week. A woman came up to me and said, "I have to tell you, I haven't had anyone in my house for over a year because I shot a home intruder in my house a year ago. I didn't kill him, but this whole year has been about court dates and lawyers and I have been so unhappy. Tonight was the first night that I actually had people in my house and it was the people who are dear to me, and you filled my house with laughter. I really feel as if you blessed my home with all my friends here." Then she started to cry and then I started to cry and I came home with that and thought *this is why I do what I do.* Because if I can touch those people, while I'm selling a really good product, that makes me feel really good, like I'm making a difference in their lives. If they can come for forty-five minutes and if they're going through a divorce, or they have a sick kid at home, for forty-five minutes they can forget about that. And on days when there's not much to laugh about, you can walk out feeling good.

CHAPTER 8

Fifty Shades of Drag

Dressing in drag, by the way, doesn't spill over into any other part of my life. I have a lot of followers on Facebook, not because I have thousands of personal friends, but because I'm trying to build a fan base. So one person contacted me—a man—and he was just fascinated with me. I knew as soon as he started asking questions that I was facing a really weird situation. You see, there's a huge difference between drag queens, transgendered individuals and transvestites. People get confused when they come to see me because they'll say, oh *I've never met a transgender before*, and I immediately correct them. I'm not a transvestite, that is, a man who enjoys dressing up in women's clothing. I am a character who puts this on, like Milton Berle and, later, Flip Wilson did. I play this character, and when I take her all off at night, there's somebody else sitting in the room…it's Kevin. I'm very different from that person. There's essences of Kevin in Dee W. Ieye, and she's taller and has bigger hair, but I don't go to the supermarket like that and I don't hang out in bars. My intention is not to go to a bar and pick up straight men. That is not what I do. I know that there are individuals out there with that intention, they fool you, they dress up like a pretty girl, they look like a pretty girl and they go man-hunting. But that's not me, that's not what I do. I play a character. I think many people come to my parties with the misconception of who I am.

I don't think that their intentions are necessarily malicious, but they just aren't educated. I can only imagine what kind of conversations some of the husbands have with their wives who book me for their parties! I show up to their houses as Kevin, so if the husbands are still there, they meet Kevin, they meet the businessman. And the women who stay late enough at the party get to meet Kevin, because all of the Dee stuff comes off before I leave. I don't go out like that. And maybe that's when I break stereotypes, because while they know that I'm a gay man, they see that I'm just playing a character and that not all gay men dress in drag.

While I'm not out to educate the public, but to entertain them, sometimes the opportunities just crop up. One morning the phone rang and a friend said, "Turn on the radio, they're talking about you!" So I did, and there were the two hosts of the show talking about someone who did a Tupperware show in drag, who looked like Dolly Parton. Well, that *had* to be me! So I listened to the show and heard them call me a transgender, asking, "Have you ever been to a transgender Tupperware party?" And they're talking about me! Now wait a minute! They were completely misrepresenting me! So I called in. When the screener heard it was me, he put me right through to the on-air line. They asked if I was the transgender drag queen who sells over $200,000 of Tupperware a year. I said, "Well, I'm not transgender, I still have all my man parts!" So in the couple of minutes on the air, at least I got my point across, got some good PR, and was able to assure them and all the people within the sound of my voice that I still possessed everything God gave me!

When I first started to do drag and my agent was sending me out for all sorts of parts, I realized that there's a whole broad spectrum of drag. When you say *drag queen,* that brings up certain mental images. Everyone has his or her own image of what a drag queen looks like. There's camp drag, and then there are men who really look like women. I'm more campy than anything else because I'm not trying to pass. I'm actor Kevin Farrell who plays a character called Dee W. Ieye. So if I'm going to go on auditions as a *she,* it needs to be as Dee. She's her own image, her own brand, and I just can't go out as second drag queen from the left—unless the second drag queen from the left is Dee W. Ieye. I'm not going to dress up as some other woman, because it's Dee or nothing.

A couple of years ago, there was a scripted show that was being shopped around with me as Dee, but the writers wanted me to be more like a real woman. They wanted the essence of Dee, but they wanted to change her look, soften her, change her hair, so that when you saw her, you thought, *hmmm…is that a guy or a girl?* Without those lashes and that loud blue eye shadow and those pink lips, there is no Dee. It would be too different and it made me uncomfortable. I worked so hard to make her who she is, I really didn't want to change her.

She has changed, of course, over the years. I have a friend who had pictures from an event from about six years ago when I did a fund raiser in Newport Beach, California, and I couldn't believe how much she (Dee) has changed! Her body's changed, her makeup has changed subtly, her hair has gone from frizzy perm to big curls. She has signature clothes. They're not J. C. Penney off the rack anymore. Every once in a while, I just shake up her wardrobe so that I don't get bored with her trademark Tupperware clothing. It's at those outside events and fund raisers that I get to wear flirty dresses and gowns that we can have some fun with.

I'm often asked if Tupperware has any problem with all this. When Jeff Sumner, the first guy to sell in drag, started a number of years ago, I heard they had a big problem with it…until he started to sell like mad. Then along came the two guys who preceded me, Oscar Quintero and Kris Andersson, and they said, *oh great, here are two more,* but THEY started to sell tons of Tupperware too! So by the time I got here, they were fine with it. I'm reaching a client base that many Tupperware ladies would never touch, so I've branched out and found a whole new audience for an established product line. People who might not go to other

Tupperware parties show up to see the "balloon clown," as we call her, and we've increased the party attendance from an average of six or eight people, to upwards of twenty-five or thirty or more. I'm in front of more people each week than many representatives are in a month. That's huge. And we're still carrying the Tupperware brand! You know, a lot of people are surprised to hear that Tupperware is still around, and that just upsets me, because I really love Tupperware, and I love my job, I believe in this company and I believe in this product. I don't drag their name in the dirt. I talk about how great Tupperware is and how much better it is than any other plastic storage products you can buy. It's an institution and it's been around more than sixty years. So this is a spin on something old that made it new!

There are Tupperware ladies out there who are not happy with what we're doing—the other Tupperware drag queens and myself. They're just not happy. Tupperware gets the phone calls. *You have to stop them from what they're doing.* But the president of Tupperware says no, without saying *hey, they're outselling you!* We're such a broad spectrum of Tupperware consultants, why can't we all be different? We can all take tips from each other and apply them to our own businesses. And the people who don't like the way I sell Tupperware don't have to come! But I don't think it's my obligation to rub their faces in what I do, so that's why when I go to the Tupperware conventions, I don't dress up in drag and run across the stage in front of 3000 Tupperware ladies as my character, unless it's during what they call "Fun Nights." There's a time and a place for me to do what I do and that was a big learning curve for me. If you don't like what I do, it's not necessary for me to smear it in your face.

Now I must admit that Tupperware executives have not attended my live presentations, but they've certainly seen me enough on the Internet to know what I do, complete with bawdy language. No one has ever told me not to do what I do or to change it. I think as a performer, I know what is appropriate and what is not. Once I drop that first f-bomb, that's testing the water. And I think that because I apologize for it and I laugh—it's all about the delivery—I can see what will work for each audience. I can determine the boundary and I know not to step over that line. I know not to talk about religion or race nor would I pick someone out in the room and make an example of that person. It makes me uncomfortable as a performer so I'm not going to do that in my show.

CHAPTER 9

You Know
I'm a Dude, Right?

I love the reactions I get from guys. Once they get over the initial shock and know I am just an actor in a wig playing a part, they fall into the show. I love it. And I really enjoy it if they stay after to meet me as Kevin, once I put Dee away for the night.

Dee has a likable appeal. I've never been able to put my finger on it. I am not trying to fool anyone. I am not trying to pass as a woman. I'm not trying to fool a guy into thinking I am a woman trying to make a move on him. So I think that is where I step around other drag queens and am able to set new boundaries. On occasion, though, those lines can get pretty blurry!

I was booked to do a party in Garden Grove, California. It was weird because I got there and I wasn't anticipating that men would be there, because ninety percent of my business is from women, but I never really know. So I showed up and heard that the husbands were going to hang out in the back and drink beer while the show was going on, but some of them hung out in the kitchen and they watched the show. The husband of the hostess had met me before—as Kevin—because I show up as Kevin. He was asking me all sorts of questions about my business like how I got started in this and how well I do—all sorts of questions about the business aspect of what I do, not about the drag business, but the *business* business. So I chatted with him as Kevin, and then he took the kids and went bowling.

Later, when they came back, they saw me as Dee, sitting at the table taking the orders. It was really hard for him to make that connection that I was the same person he was talking to earlier, in a baseball cap and jeans, putting the Tupperware out on the table. Now I'm in hot pants and heels and legs for days. The kids had met me as Kevin, too, and the two little girls stood right next to my right elbow, watching every move I made. They were fascinated with me, uh, Dee.

The husband had had a few beers while he was bowling with the kids, so he was a little bit looser than during our original conversation. He was just making comments from his spot over in the corner, like *look at that ass, look at those legs, and she's so hot*—comments like that. Now he wasn't saying it to me, but I could hear him over my shoulder. Understand that it's very odd for me to be in character, a boy in drag, and hear the comments from the men, because that's not my intention. I'm not there to arouse anyone or get comments or wolf whistles from anyone and it's just that I want to say, *hey, you know I'm a dude, right? You met me earlier, I'm a dude.*

What's even funnier is that I'm very active in the gay and lesbian community, and when the lesbians come up to me when I'm dressed as Dee, that's even more weird, because the lesbians are coming on to me and checking me out as a chick and I want to say, *you know I'm a guy dressed as a woman, I'm not really a girl!* There's one lesbian in particular, an acquaintance of mine who I used to run into a lot, and every time she saw me in drag, it's like she wanted to take me out, she wanted to date me! And she'd even make comments on Facebook...*you're one hot chick, maybe we can go out sometime.* I just wanted to say, *Karen, really?*

They may know me as Kevin, but they somehow have a disconnect and it's just fascinating to me. Because there's such a difference between Kevin, the actor and Dee W. Ieye, the Tupperware personality or whatever she is that night, they just don't make the connection. So I guess I'm doing my job because people look at pictures of Kevin while I'm dressed at Dee, and say that can't be you! You're so different. And I say yeah, *you wouldn't recognize me at Walmart!* One girl looked at a picture of me as Kevin and said, "He's cute," and I said, "Thanks, I'll tell him."

Before I was able to do business as Dee, all the Tupperware checks had to be made out to Kevin Farrell, so I always had a picture next to me at the order table with the correct spelling of my name, and I would ask people to just make their checks out to "my accountant, Kevin Farrell." That was my stock answer until I established a business account where "Dee" could accept checks made out to "her." For the longest time, people really thought that was my accountant, and it wasn't until later when I was on Facebook that they found out it was really me. So it was pretty funny. It's all very confusing and there are times I can't wait to get home so I can just be Kevin again.

CHAPTER 10

Making Up
is Hard to Do!

Some girls have such large guest lists for their Tupperware parties that their homes can't accommodate the crowd, so they wind up renting out a clubhouse or the activities room in their condo complex or in the local senior citizens center. And I've done a lot of bars, especially in Columbus, Ohio, where a bar may close down entirely for us on a Saturday or Sunday afternoon. Sometimes, bathrooms become a problem, however, even when there's one men's room and one ladies' room.

One time, we were doing a party in the community center of a mobile home complex, and there were two restrooms, one for men and one for women. I was obviously in the men's room, and we'd put a sign on the door saying "out of order." I was standing there putting my makeup on, dressed as a boy, face as a girl, and a guy walked into the bathroom. I just HATE those situations, like *hey dude*…I mean, it's not only embarrassing for me, but I'm embarrassed for them because all of a sudden it's, like, what the hell was THAT? Not the best scenario. I've done a lot of bars, too, and I'll get ready in the bathroom, hoping that nobody comes in, but I've even gotten ready in the liquor closet, where I sit with my mirror propped up against a carton of Absolut, trying to put my makeup on with the beer taps running.

So I've seen it all, including athletic clubs where they'll put me in the manager's office, where I have a private room but with no mirror and poor lighting, and I have to make sure that when I strip down to my skivvies to put on Dee's pantyhose, nobody comes popping in the door!

I routinely tell hostesses that it takes me forty-five minutes to do my makeup during which you are free to come knock on the door and ask me a question, but there's a very small window when NOBODY should be coming in because trust me, NO ONE wants to see me in that state! That's when it gets a little bit scary, so we have to be careful about that!

CHAPTER 11

Let's PARTY!

When I walk into a room, my normal reception is, "Oh my God, she's HERE!" The roof lifts off the house and it's pandemonium! We get the party started and it's energy, energy, energy and fun, fun, fun! But there have been times when I've walked into a room and people look up at me as if I look like everybody else and you can practically see the collective SHRUG...well, thank God that doesn't happen very often! If they're not ecstatic to see me, that's when I feel like a freak. Those are the times that make me feel like *what am I doing, why am I here,* because if you don't jump out of your seat when you see me—I mean, how could you not—when I don't get that response, it's like somebody throws a big bucket of cold water on me. Those times are the WORST, because I come in ready to entertain. I have a lot of energy when I'm in front of a group talking to them as Dee W. Ieye, so when I walk into a room and the response is less than adequate, I feel, like, *Ugh!*

Now, I can usually save the situation, but I have to pull energy from the tiniest cuticle of my little baby toe and, as a performer, it's tough. Once I was doing a party along with a friend who was there selling designer flip-flops. I figured *hey, I'm in front of a large group of people, I have a captive audience, bring your flip-flops and let's sell some stuff.* So I walk out into a room of about thirty-five girls, and the response is just flat. It's a total flat line, nobody even had a pulse. So I walked into the other room and said to my friend Stacy, "What's going on?" She said, "I don't know, that's really weird, everybody just didn't respond to you." So I regrouped, went back in and did my show and it took me about ten minutes to get 'em. They were slow to get on the train with me, but I persevered, and finally they were all laughing and having a great time, but it was those first ten minutes that were like pulling teeth. I came to find out later when I was chatting with the hostess that she had planned my appearance as a SURPRISE! Nobody knew I was coming! That is a HUGE mistake and had I known that was her intention, we would have had a serious conversation beforehand, because these poor people had ten minutes of being in total shock, like *what the hell is THAT?*

They knew they were coming to a Tupperware party,

but they thought I was going to be a regular Tupperware lady, and Grandma was there from New York. Old World, Italian grandmother was sitting in the front row, I'm doing my show, and she is looking at me as if she wants to string me up. So I finish the show, and when I was sitting at the table taking orders, she came over to the table and sat down next to me. And I thought, *OK, here we go*…but she touched me on the hand and said, "I have never had so much fun in my entire life!" And she sat there, telling me every piece of Tupperware she'd had in her kitchen for her whole life, as a child, and raising her own family. She told me stories, gave me recipes, it was amazing. And that's when I started to learn that I could cross boundaries with this character in ways few people can. I cross boundaries with age and race and sexual orientation…it's just amazing.

At another party, when my cousin Ginger was with me, two little ladies came in late and there was no place to sit, so the hostess brought out two folding chairs and sat them right in front of me, so close I could have reached out and touched them. They were somewhere north of seventy-five years old, and they sat there stone-faced with me dropping the f-bomb and all the other things I say. My cousin said, "Didn't you see the two ladies sitting in the front row?" (*How could I have missed them? They were right there in front of me!*) "Well," she said, "they were NOT diggin' you!" I felt terrible. I said I knew that, but everyone else was already having such a good time when they came in, it would have been hard to switch gears in mid-show.

Fast-forward to about three days later. I was talking to

the hostess and I tried to apologize. "I'm really sorry about those two ladies in the front row," I said, and she said, "Oh my God, they CANNOT stop talking about you!" *What?* "That was my Aunt Sophie and her good friend, and they are absolutely obsessed with you. They've been calling and saying how funny you are, quoting your jokes and saying they couldn't remember when they'd had such a good time!" Well, you could have hammered me to the wall because the way they looked at me during the show, I thought they wanted to skin me alive!

CHAPTER 12

Mama Said There'd Be Days Like This!

I've learned you can never judge how people will react. Sometimes, they arrive with ingrained attitudes that I'm not going to change in forty-five minutes. I had a lady walk out of my show once. It was a beautiful Sunday afternoon, and I was on the back porch and this woman sat right in the front row. She knew what she was coming to. I was about five minutes into my show and she stood up from the front row, turned and walked all the way to the back and just walked out. I was able to save it with a joke—not at the woman's expense, but at mine—and everyone had a good laugh, but I felt terrible. Later on, the hostess told me that the woman had seen my picture, knew what she was coming to, but when she got there, she just couldn't handle it, so that was that.

The only other time anything like that happened was in Marysville, Ohio, where a reporter was there doing an article on me. Sitting there in the front row (why are they always in the front row?) were two women who just didn't seem to be having a good time. So I just went on with the show and tried not to think about it. They never came to the table to place an order, so I never saw them again that evening. After everyone left, we were picking up catalogs and discovered that on a piece of notebook paper I had supplied, one women had written a letter to me about how inappropriate I was and listed the jokes I made that they didn't like. She had started the whole letter by saying, "I'm not a prude, but..." and you know what? That really hurt my feelings. It took me a couple of days to get over that. I mean, they looked like they could be my aunts. The reason I think it hurt my feelings is that I don't do this to offend anybody, I do this so that people can laugh and have a good time. I took the note to the hostess because I was so offended that they slipped the letter into my catalogue and didn't even have a face-to-face conversation with me. *I'm going to tell you how much I hate you, but I'm not going to say it to your face.* The hostess tried to apologize for them, but I just wanted to know why they were there in the first place. They knew about the show and had seen a picture. I'm not sure what they were expecting! Here's the funny thing. One of the women owned the local ice cream parlor in Marysville and she got quoted in the article that the reporter was writing and was identified as the owner of that business! So SHE got the publicity from the article about ME by saying how much she hated me. "You're welcome."

So I'm not everyone's cup of tea, and that's OK, I just wish they had stayed home once they found what the show was about rather than put everyone through all that discomfort. I try to do damage control as much as possible, because this is not an experience suitable for kids. I remember a party when a girl showed up with her eight-year-old daughter and, once again, sat right in the front row. You could feel everyone in the room just tense up to see what I was going to do with a little kid sitting right up front. And you know what? They got the G-rated version. I cleaned it up, they got a totally different show and nobody was the wiser except my partner, who was listening from another room, and the hostess who had seen the show before. She later apologized and said she had no idea that the girl had planned to bring a youngster to a show she had clearly warned was adults-only. But everyone still had a good time.

CHAPTER 13

I'm an
Act-*or*

I wasn't sure George and I were going to meet—or that he was going to meet Dee—he had said he was going to stay in his office and keep pretty much to himself while the party was going on. His wife, the hostess, explained that George was pretty straight-laced and reserved, so I thought interacting with Dee might be kind of a stretch for him. But before I had a chance to change back into civvies, he came around the corner and he just looked at me and said, "Hi. How'd it go?" I thought one of us was going to have a stroke. It was fun. Because I show up as Kevin to parties, if I get a chance to meet the husbands before they leave with the kids or go drinking with the boys because they don't want to be in the house with all the Tupperware girls, they get a chance to meet Kevin. I like that because I think some people have a preconceived notion of what is coming into their house because of the picture they've seen, and when they get to meet Kevin, who is kind of the guy next door, a down-to-earth businessman, they are then able to make that connection that I'm not a sexual deviant. It's an air of normalcy.

I've always professed to be an actor who plays a character, not a drag queen. Now I could argue that point until the cows come home. I'm an actor who plays this character, and I play no other character. I don't perform in clubs, I don't pole-dance for dollar bills tucked into my bustier. As for myself and the other guys who do this, we are all creative men, trudging the road of the actor's life and doing what we have to do to be an actor to support ourselves in our respective cities.

Look, I didn't move to California to be a drag queen at all, I moved there to be an actor and that was in 1996 when I went out there to do that episode of *Frasier* and I decided to stay. So I moved my little one bedroom apartment from Chicago out to California, I shot that episode and started to do all sorts of little guest spots building on that episode. I got an agent and manager out of it. I got a lot of press out of it. And that worked for about six years. But I was always looking for the next gig, the next role, because I was never a regular or had a recurring role on a TV show. I was always just looking for the next thing. And it was really hard, because I think for anybody who's really, really good at what they do, anybody who is really a creative person, it's hard to hold jobs at an office running a copy machine or serving somebody some mackerel on a Wednesday night. I did all of those things and I appreciated it for what it was at the time, but it wasn't what I wanted to do.

There's something that happens inside of me when I'm standing in front of a group of people and I'm doing what I feel I was put on this planet to do, and that's to make people laugh. I used to do it as Kevin the actor but I found a way to do it even more successfully as this character, as Dee W. Ieye, and after I started to really get her voice and feel who she was as a real person, it just became more and more natural to be her, to talk as her, to have conversations as her. She's a totally different person, a character that I play. But it was so nice to find something as an actor, becoming a present-day *Tootsie,* so that I was able to reinvent myself as an actor and not rely on other people for a job. I didn't have to go on auditions anymore with eighteen other actors who all looked different—for five lines on an ABC sitcom some of whom I recognized from having done a LOT of work—I couldn't believe I was sitting in a room with Nathan Lane or some guy who was on a hit show in 1999 who everyone knows, and all of a sudden I had to complete with those guys because THEY were out of work and they were showing up to do five lines on a sitcom!

Hollywood is a tough town to live in. For the longest time I felt that was where I wanted to be but now I feel as if I can be anywhere and still available to work in L.A. I've done interviews and auditions on Skype so if anybody wants me, I'm a plane ride away and in the meantime, I can enjoy the sanity and sanctity of the Midwest.

CHAPTER 14

Stop Talking — I'm Working Here!

It's always an issue in larger parties where I will get the little talkers. The ones who can't keep their mouths shut. Just rude. They are the ones who probably talk through movies and plays and disturb those around them. I've often gotten these parties where it is just so hard to keep the extra talk to a minimum. I hate having to stop my show and give them a talking to. And since I never like to drop character, I have to do it as Dee (with Kevin under the wig raging and trying not to kill them). It's a delicate balance because I never want to take the chance to have the whole room turn on me and then it's me against forty-five hostile women who think I am the rude one. I mean, seriously, you do not have to listen to me, but for God's sake, take it outside. If you really need to talk about Bobby's soccer injury or your new boob job, do it out of my show and don't ruin it for others who came to actually pay attention. *Geeez.*

Anyway—the worst of the worst happened recently in Hilliard, Ohio. I was doing a show at the Bag of Nails, a bar/restaurant that has a private party room. Nice room, but it was summer and their air conditioning wasn't working efficiently. It was hotter than the hinges to hell. I am on stage on a raised platform with about twelve large round banquet tables surrounding me. I figure there were about twenty-five people in the room. It seemed like less since they were spread out throughout the room with only a few at each table.

This is my fifth party in as many days. It's hot, I'm tired, I'm done. My level of acceptance of anything that I would find disturbing or unacceptable is zero. So I am about fifteen minutes into my show and my eye keeps falling on these two girls sitting at a table by themselves off to the left in full conversation. Not just not paying little attention to me—but completely ignoring me. I mean, the one girl talking had her chair completely turned away from the stage and her back was to me. I snapped. I admit it. I wasn't rude, but I stopped completely. I got their attention and mentioned that it was difficult to do what I was doing with their conversation going on. Well, they reacted like I threw hot wax on them. Shocked. OMG! Kinda like when you used to get caught by the teacher for screwing around during class.

They stopped momentarily. About five minutes later, the major offender got up and left, leaving the one girl by herself. That girl came to me afterward to apologize. She was mortified. Story was (and actually I didn't really care) she met the major offender just the other night at another party. They were not really friends. Major offender, it seems, was going through a divorce and I guess found it OK to hash out her divorce problems during my Tupperware show to a complete stranger. So, Major Offender—if you are reading this—congratulations…you got in print for being rude at a private Tupperware presentation. Sorry for your divorce experience, but next time choose a better time and place to ask for advice, like maybe over coffee, at Starbucks. Or on the phone, in your own home. Invite me over so I can do something in your kitchen that is really annoying that will totally distract you and unhinge your conversation.

68

CHAPTER 15

My Favorite Party— Reader Discretion Advised!

There's a theater company in Covina, California where I've twice been invited to come and perform at their company fund-raisers. They have a beautiful theater, a terrific stage, great dressing rooms, and, best of all, I get to be on stage—and I LOVE to be on the stage of an actual theater. The first time I performed there, they held a little mixer beforehand. I went out as Dee W. Ieye and I was being introduced to all the people there in the bar area, including one woman who must have been in her late eighties.

She was like the matriarch of Covina. When I was introduced to her she was very polite, very nice, very quiet and demure. When I took the stage, I did my whole show, the way I usually do it, with an ample amount of sassy talk and cussing. A friend of mine who works for Tupperware had come to see that show. After the show, she was standing on the corner outside the theater, smoking a cigarette, when that woman left the theater with her two cronies. Now, if she was eighty-something, her friends were in their sixties. As they walked by, flanking her on either side, one of the women said, "Oh my God, I can't believe that he used that shit word." The other woman said, "Are you kidding? I can't believe that he said the F word!" And the older woman, standing between them, said, "Fuck you both. I have never had so much fun in my life!"

My friend Sharon said she almost fell off the curb laughing when she heard that coming from the mouth of that little old lady, the matriarch of Covina. I just love that story because it tells me that little old woman came to my party and had a good time, and she just told her friends to go F themselves if they didn't like it. So there you go. You know, I'm not everybody's cup of tea but you know what, the people who come and have a good time, that's what I want them to go home with. And that's my favorite story.

CHAPTER 16

Let's Swing!

Not so long ago I was approached by a woman in Columbus, Ohio, who asked if I did co-ed parties. I said yes, of course. I did, however, mention that was important that the men in attendance must have a sense of humor and not have a problem with the way I present my show. She said fine. No problem. But I didn't hear from her for the longest time.

Finally, after about a year, I was surprised to find this girl on the other end of the phone and we start actually planning her party. When she tells me there will be twenty-four people there, I say, *if this is a co-ed party* and these are "couples," that would mean ONE order per couple—so really there would be twelve people in attendance. I am not convinced she gets me. So I explain the whole idea that I am a salesperson and entertainer—I sell Tupperware, I take orders, and twenty-four couples actually means twelve orders. Still not sure she's getting me....

OK—so I get to the party and I walk out to do my show and I immediately get a feeling in my stomach I never had in all the years I've been working as Dee. All couples. All sitting in little groups. Exactly twenty-four people (twelve orders ringing in my head). I do my show. I have one guy who is an amazing jerk who keeps heckling me and trying to get his own laughs. NOT someone I like at a party. Three girls standing in the kitchen, carrying on a conversation the whole time like they were at the water cooler at the office, paying no attention to me whatsoever. They weren't really bothering the group, thank God, since they were far enough away from the group, but I could see them—they were in my direct line of vision.

So I do the party, I have my order helpers in the dining room, we leave with exactly twelve orders, as I had predicted. The show barely makes the $1,000 in retail mark, far below my norm for that number of people so, needless to say, I am disappointed. But here is the clincher—remember that funny feeling I had early in the evening? Well, after the party, it finally hit me. This was not just a co-ed party...this was a SWINGERS party. We swing, and swap spouses. WHAT?! Are you kidding me? This is a first.

My friend who was visiting me at the time called it a

punch bowl party—where the husbands throw their keys in a punch bowl, the women pick out keys and leave with whomever owns the keys they grab. SERIOUSLY?

Now I really am not one to judge. But I will say from the looks of the dudes in that room—I didn't want their keys! And if I had gotten the heckler's keys, well let's just say he would have found 'em where the sun don't shine!

Chalk another one up to the "I've never done that kind of party before" category!

CHAPTER 17

Zanesville, Ohio

I'm very big on traveling. I'll go wherever people want me as long as there is an understanding that making sales is the goal and if I travel a long distance and we don't hit the sales we want—and agree on it ahead of time—there may be a charge for my show.

One night, I was approached by a lovely lady at a party in Grove City, Ohio, who wanted me to travel to Zanesville. Since Zanesville is about ninety minutes from my home, I was quick to explain that we needed a guarantee of at least fifty people for me to travel there and that we had an expectation of high sales. She said *no problem*.

While I grew up in Columbus, Ohio, I had never been to Zanesville. On the night of the party, I drove out to do her show. She had told me it would be at a local bar called The Grinning Sheep (name changed to protect the innocent) and that she'd have about sixty guests in attendance. I arrived in plenty of time to set up. From the outside, the bar looked to be a bit rough and tumble and in an area of Zanesville where there were some colorful pedestrians and the surrounding buildings had boarded up windows. I thought *OK...here we go!*

The hostess arrived—again, lovely and gracious. I got all set up. She'd brought tons of food. The place was packed when I came out to do the show. They were loud, fun and ready to party. It was 1 o'clock in the afternoon.

The kegs were flowing, shots were being passed and we were ready to party. We had great sales—$2,600. The crowd got a bit drunk, and at the end, one girl took a spill into a table full of drinks and broke all the glasses. She was fine, though, and popped right back up and continued dancing. My order taker-assistants were a bit scared of the surroundings when they first arrived (I take helpers with me at larger parties). We laughed later because one of them always carries a gun with her. I thought it funny that Dee's order takers have to "pack heat" sometimes, depending on the areas we travel into. Makes me feel safe.

So one more time, I never know where I am going end up on this Tupperware journey!

CHAPTER 18

Expect
the Unexpected!

Every few months there's a new Tupperware product featured and every thirty days there are new sales specials, so I try to incorporate these specials into the show. I may write jokes associated with the new items but I basically have a structure to my show that I've done for the past nine years. I have Dee's backstory down pat so she tells her story about how she got into Tupperware, she gives a bit of the history of Tupperware, and then she launches into the catalogue, which includes six to ten regular items that I show along with whatever sales specials are on at that time. Some shows are a little bit longer than others, some are a bit harder to produce, so it's a constant balancing act for me as a salesperson and as a performer. I have to keep the body of the show and the jokes that work, the jokes that are associated with the products sold on an ongoing basis, plus I have to come up with new material for the specials that are only around for thirty days. There is, however, a certain amount of ad libbing coming from Dee's reaction to the audience or something happening in the room, someone's cell phone going off, or unexpected children coming into the room.

I wish there had been a camera on my face the night I heard little voices come through the front door. I stopped in my tracks and said, "Oh shit...children!" The whole audience just peed in their pants. And that, for a performer, is just gold. There's nothing better than that. I could spend hours trying to write a joke and it would not be as funny as when something like that happens. They just knew... there were kids who were walking through the front door and there was this seven-foot drag queen in the middle of the living room. *Lucy! You've got some splainin' to do!*

When things like that happen, I just love it. I was doing a show one night and I was facing the front door with everyone else faced toward me. So I could see everyone coming in the front door. Well, this house had one of those *"invisi-screens"*—a retractable screen door—on the front door. Three people came up to the front door and walked smack into the screen...and I just lost it.

One night, I did a party in Laguna Hills, California, and I walked out and there were these two girls who were about 15 or 16 sitting there, and they looked at me like, *what the hell are you, what are you going to do, prove it, bring it.* I could tell when I looked at them that they just had the biggest attitude about me, as big an attitude as my hair! Well, halfway through the show, I picked them out and dropped a joke on them, and they snickered. And then they laughed. And as they got more comfortable with what was going on, they bought into it. By the end of the show, they loved Dee and just had to have their picture taken with me! So it never fails that during almost any show, I can find a way to soften the hardest glare, and unhinge the most ardent preconceived notion people have of what they're going to see. They don't know quite what to expect when they hear it's a drag queen, but the truth is I'm an actor who dresses up like a woman to sell Tupperware. That's what I do.

It's like the grandma who looked at me with a sour puss as if she wished I would burst into flames on the spot, and wound up sitting with me at the end of the show sharing recipes with me. I think she wanted to adopt me, and I loved that feeling. It just makes me feel good.

CHAPTER 19

Sometimes Life's a Bust!

Not long ago, I did a party for a woman who works for another direct selling company, which shall remain nameless, after having been to one of her parties. She found out who I was and wanted to do a party. I gave her the parameters for my party and she agreed. She had thirty people come to a restaurant-bar, a nice venue I've played before, and I did my show and it turned out to be a $400 show. Out of thirty people there, I came home with nine paper orders. At the end of the show, I went to take off my makeup and change my clothes while Geoff added up the orders and gave the hostess the total, and she knew the party was a bust. We didn't have any awkward moment, though, because I was so tired, I just wanted to get out of there and I told her I'd call her the next day. This was another example of trying to figure out why this happens and what we can do to make sure I get paid for what I do and nights like this don't happen again.

I came home from that party and was just beside myself. I thought, I have to start doing what I did in LA...I have to start charging for my show. If we don't reach a certain amount in sales, I have to charge something, a flat fee or a sliding scale. I made a hundred bucks that night, and I have set the value of my show at $350 for what I do. At first I thought, *well, Columbus ain't LA and the sales can't compare*, except that they DO and they HAVE! But nights like that are a complete and total waste of my time and considerable energy it takes to put on this elaborate makeup, and getup, and show! It just makes me angry, because while there's no obligation to buy anything, that night thirty people came and more than two-thirds of them bought NOTHING! The hostess was as horrified as I was. As a direct seller, she knew how bad it was. I had to think about the show. Was it different? Was I off? And the answer was NO...people laughed and cheered, everybody loved it. It was just that nobody opened their checkbooks!

So every now and then one of those sneaks in on me... even though I try really, really hard to make sure that doesn't happen, because that just makes me feel as if I've put myself out there and wound up with the crappy end of the stick.

A lot of people feel that they shouldn't have to pay for a

Tupperware party, and I say, *well, nice chattin' with you, go find yourself a Tupperware lady!* If they want Dee W. Ieye, that's the way it has to be. I don't think it's unreasonable. That was probably my worst party except for the first party I did when I got to Columbus when three people showed up on a Sunday afternoon in April. I was all dolled up as Dee and while I didn't do my whole show, I went into my schtick. There were three adult women there and their assorted teenage girls, bringing the audience total to about seven. I tried really hard not to let my anger show. I didn't sing, I didn't go on and on, I just got on and got off.

CHAPTER 20

Never Again!

People often ask me about the most outrageous party I've ever encountered, and there have been plenty, but here's one I would not care to experience again. I have expectations as to how many people are going to be at my parties and I plan carefully with my hostesses. We have to have x-amount of people, we have to sell x-amount of product and we enter into a verbal contract with one another in order to get me to come into their homes as an entertainer. So this woman who lived out in Riverside, California, more than an hour-and-a-half drive from L.A. proper, had promised me that she was going to have more than thirty people at her party. As I always do, I started calling my hostess days before, *Hey, I'm coming on Friday. Do you have your people? Oh yes, yes...everyone's so excited,* she said. Then I called on Thursday and said, "You know I'm coming a really long way. You have your people, right?" *Oh, yes, everyone's really excited* was the reply.

So Geoff went with me and we got to the house, a little itty-bitty house in Riverside, and I walked in to see her and two girlfriends who were setting up for the party. I set up my tables and said, "So you have a lot of people coming, right?" *Oh yeah, yeah...*and then I went into the master bathroom to get ready. This bathroom has a window that looks right out on to the front porch so I could see if people approached the front door because it was in the summertime and the window was open. I started my makeup an hour before people are supposed to arrive and NO ONE was showing up! Geoff is in the other room playing Angry Birds on his telephone and I'm in denial. I can usually judge the success of a party by hearing people arrive. Doorbell rings, people are laughing. Bell rings again, more people, more talking and laughing.

That night, NOTHING.

So I get all my makeup on and by this time, no one has approached the front door for this party. I get dressed and I turned to Geoff and said, "You want to go out there and see what's going on?" He went out and came back in and said that there was no one there except for the people who were there when we first arrived, but the hostess was frantically on the phone making phone calls. There were four people in a car that was just getting off the freeway.

That was it. The car pulled up and four girls got out and came in and it was time for me to go and do my show. And you know what? If Geoff hadn't been there to be the voice of reason, I really don't know what I would have done. I was pissed. It was a ninety-minute drive in the middle of summer, I was going to sell squat, and I heard one of the women say, "I don't know why I'm at a Tupperware party. I don't have any money." So for me as a performer, to be excited to walk out of that bedroom, dressed as I'm dressed, put on a show, and have four people there and hear THAT before I go out, I thought *I do not want to be here, I'd rather be home on my couch, I'd rather be out to dinner with friends, I'd rather be painting my living room, I'd rather be doing ANYTHING but be here right now.* But Geoff came in and he gave me some advice. He said, "I overheard the hostess say that this was her housewarming party, so you have to go out there and do your show for these four people." So I went out and did an abbreviated version of my act and talked about four pieces of Tupperware. Geoff had said, "You know, I feel sorry for this woman. This is her housewarming party and no one showed up. When you and I have a party, people show up to our house. Go out there, give them a little Dee W. Ieye and then we'll pack up and go home." So that's what I did.

Occasionally, I take older products or older colors of some products and sell them at a discounted price, which I did on that night. I think I sold $200 from the catalogue but they bought every single discounted piece from my cash-and-carry table and that money went right into my pocket to pay for my gas to drive all the way out to Riverside. But I would never want to repeat that! In fact, that's when I started to implement my whole booking policy where I charge $100 if we don't meet a certain goal. That was one of the first parties when I said no more of this, someone needs to be responsible for my time and travel expense. Not a fun night.

CHAPTER 21

Doggies and Birdies and Kiddies, Oh My!

Whenever there are kids involved, I always worry about how things are explained to them. Most of them have seen pictures of me as Dee and they can't wait until the Tupperware lady gets there! They're usually lined up at the door to see me when I show up, and are so disappointed when I walk in as Kevin, which I always do. Little kids are usually in the way, so Dad takes them somewhere else during the Tupperware show. But when they come back after the show, there I am, Dee in full regalia, and I get everything from *AAH! Who's THAT?* to *Who's the big pretty lady?* In a perfect world, there would be no children to deal with at parties and no barking dogs either. I can't tell you how many times I've been in a house where the door opens and I get knocked over by a fleet of animals or they lock them in a room and they bark nonstop. Now I can block noises in my head for a time, but after a while it's like fingernails on a chalkboard.

I was down in Rolling Hills Estates, California, one evening where the hostess had a house that could not accommodate everybody. So we set up out on the back porch, where she must have had six or seven bird cages with exotic birds. Well, these birds made all kinds of noise, with the ringleader being this cockatoo in his cage who did not like that everybody was invading his domain. Plus, he really did not like the fact that the hostess—his mama—had her attention being drawn away from him. He would SCREAM, like something I'd never heard before, and he got all the other birds riled up, so I started my show with this cacophony of screaming birds. I had like thirty-five women looking at me thinking, *how are you going to do this?* I actually had no idea. This was going to be a forty-minute demonstration with nonstop screaming birds!

There was nothing I could do and I had no idea how I was going to work through this. At one point, the hostess went over and stood next to the ringleader's cage. And because she stood close enough to the cage, the bird stopped screaming. But as soon as she walked even a few steps away, he would start up again. I thought *oh my God, please don't leave that birdcage, you need to stand right next to that birdcage the whole time I'm doing the show.* That was one of the hardest shows I ever had to get through. It was an uphill battle, I'll tell you, with me as a sole performer up against all those damn birds!

Wasn't it W.C. Fields who said he never worked with children or animals? Now I know what he was talking about!

CHAPTER 22

Heckle
&
Jeckle

I'll still take squawking birds over the women who sometimes come and decide they want to be the entertainment at my Tupperware shows! Professional Tupperware hecklers! I can't do anything about those women...I just wish there were someone to stand next to THEIR cages so that they would SHUT UP! I won't drop character to handle it and I can't turn on them and risk others in the room getting mad. So I have to grin and bear it or try to make some kind of comment. I've had school teachers tell me to go right up and stand next to them like they do to second-graders who are misbehaving. My father thought it would be funny if I had one of those little cricket clickers and I could just *click click click* while I kept talking. I actually bought one, but as many times as I had it on my table, I never had occasion to use it. Too bad. Now, of course, I have no idea where it is!

I've had women actually answer their phones during a demonstration. Not just turning it off if it rings, but answering it and having a conversation! That is appalling to me. Where do they think they are? I was at a party where I was training someone to do what I do and his character was a Catholic nun in drag. He went over and demanded the phone be given to him, like only a Catholic nun would do. *Sister is talking,* he said, and he took the phone and had a conversation with the person on the other end, explaining that this was the middle of Catechism class and that her friend was not available to speak…and then he hung up! It was hysterical. Sometimes I wish that my character could get away with stuff like that, but I'm always afraid to try it.

A Tupperware friend once suggested something to me. He had saved an inflatable baseball bat from a rally that said Tupperware on it. He would keep it in full view on the table in front of him and if anyone talked during his presentation he would say, *do you want Aunt Lola's naughty stick? If you don't stop talking, you're going to get hit with Aunt Lola's naughty stick!* We need some humorous way to diffuse the situation without getting totally pissed off, because there have been parties when I have been moved to such anger for the fact that I'm working my ass cheeks off up here and there's a total disregard to the fact that I'm *working…*I'm doing a show…and it's just rude.

That one party when I stopped and said, "Look, ladies, this is really difficult for me, but I cannot talk over the top of you." And they all went "Ooooo," like some petulant third graders and I thought *see, that's why I don't say anything.* So if I don't do it with humor, it just comes back to bite me in the behind. A good lesson learned, though.

I really think the responsibility lies primarily with the hostesses. If I sense that it's going to go that way, I'll take a hostess aside and say, "If this goes off the chain, if the party goes off the rails, I need you to get it back on track." And actually, when I did the party at a bar in Woodland Hills, California, it was off the rails. No one was paying any attention to me aside from a handful of people, and I was saying *Shh, please, ladies, shh, please ladies,* and then the hostess came up and said I need to speak louder because the women in the back couldn't hear me! That's when I thought my head was going to explode. I told her, I need you to tell them to stop talking because I can't scream over the top of people who were having a blast at my expense and preventing me from conveying any information to people who were going to be buying my product. So as a salesperson, that's really, really hard.

If I were just doing a show and had no other agenda, it would be a different story. If I were just being paid to perform, I'd come out, do my show, we'd all have a good time, you could talk, you could laugh, I could sit on your lap and that would be fine. But trying to sell? Not going to happen. If it's in a bar, open to the public, it just won't work with the basketball game on over my head and people at the bar doing shots, so I limit my bar performances to private parties.

I've learned these things the hard way. Believe me.

CHAPTER 23

Ho Ho Ho, Y'all!

During my very first Christmas season with Tupperware, I was very excited to do my very first Christmas Tupperware party because I wanted Dee W. Ieye to be dressed up in her Christmas regalia. So I wore this red and green outfit and I had poinsettias in my hair and I had big Christmas ornaments hanging from my ears. Oh, I was just so excited to do this Christmas Tupperware party! It was in LA's San Fernando Valley in a lovely area called Sherman Oaks. It turns out that the hostess was Jewish....and I walked out with all my little Christmas decorations on! The very first person who came up to me said, "What about Chanukah?" She just stopped me in my tracks. I had to think fast… "Chanukah?" I said. "Honey, I live in a trailer park in Tennessee, we don't have Jewish people in the trailer park." She just laughed and walked away. From that moment on, I swore I'd remember to always have something Chanukah on me when I do my Christmas parties, because you just never know.

I usually wear the same outfit all the time. I rarely venture away from my Daisy Dukes and my apron and my gingham shirt tied at my waist, but during the holiday times I try to get a little festive. I wear a little green outfit for St. Patrick's Day, but my regular outfit is easier for me to pack, easier for me to dress myself—I'm not trying to zip myself into a ball gown or anything—and it identifies me because my character is recognizable as a little bit Dolly and a little bit Ellie Mae Clampett. I didn't design her with Ellie Mae in mind, but really that's who she is, with a little bit of the chick from *Dukes of Hazzard* thrown in, kind of down-to-earth country, her signature look. It works for me…and her!

CHAPTER 24

Location, Location, Location!

About six years ago, a woman asked me to travel to San Bernardino from my suburban Los Angeles home, and that was pretty far for me to drive. I said OK, I'll come to San Bernardino, but we have to make sure we have a lot of people. She said she'd have to see what she could do because she couldn't fit them all in her house. So she came back to me around the holiday time, about a month before the party, and said she had a place that will accommodate everyone she wanted to invite but it was at the local mortuary! I thought…well, OK, maybe it's a little macabre…but it worked because she had more than eighty people there! We held the party in the "wake room"—fortunately, there were no viewings in progress at the time—and it was great. Being at the mortuary lent itself to some pretty interesting ad libs during the evening, and I was just glad there was an audience. Getting eighty people to show up for a Tupperware party at a mortuary was pretty funny in and of itself! I wore my little Christmas outfit for some holiday cheer and the party was a rousing success—more than $3000! I still communicate with that lady and always remember her as the mortuary lady. I don't take any orders from the great beyond, however, but I'd consider it if I thought the credit cards would go through!

I've also done parties in bars, where it's usually hard for me to find a place to get ready, so they generally lock me in a bathroom where nobody will have access, or in the liquor room with all the vodka bottles (kind of ironic, since I don't drink!). I've done several country clubs, where I prefer to be in a private room, but I did one recently here in Ohio where they put me in the lobby of the country club, so everyone who was coming in for whatever reason saw me standing there in the middle of the lobby. They tried to put up some partitions to give us a little privacy, and there were about forty or fifty women there who sat on folding chairs, but I prefer not to be stuck out in public, especially where there are people who don't know that there's a Tupperware party going on led by an outrageous drag queen! It makes me uncomfortable, it makes the people watching the show uncomfortable, and you know that Dee's mouth is *not* to be trusted. I had to be very cautious because of little children who kept popping up and running up the stairs to catch a glimpse of me. They were fascinated with Dee and were craning their necks to get a better view, but I had to be very careful about what was going to fly out of my mouth with children walking through the lobby. Other than that, doing a Tupperware party at a country club is a lot of fun.

CHAPTER 25

Oh, Baby!

During the first or second year of my Tupperware experience, I was doing a party down in Laguna Niguel, a lovely Southern California city. A woman came in and she was just so pregnant, so incredibly pregnant, I couldn't believe she was still walking around. She came early to say hello to the hostess and was planning to stay. I said, "Oh my God, when are you *due?*" It was within days and I thought, *okaaaay, here we go! Let's get this show on the road!*

So I'm doing the show and the woman is sitting on the couch next to her girlfriend and towards the end of the evening, I could see her starting to sink lower and lower into her seat. I could tell by her face that she was not mentally in the room. I swear this woman was going to have her baby right in the middle of my Tupperware show! I thought, *well, this will be a first!* As soon as we were done, as we were getting ready to do the orders, she and her friend popped up off of their chairs. They had their order forms filled out, and they said, "We have to GO!" They actually wanted to put their order in first! I was so flustered, I'm surprised I got the order written at all and they hurried off to the hospital, or so I thought. A short time later, as I was breaking down the show and packing up my boxes, they walked through the door! It turned out to be a false alarm...but I thought *how funny was that, if her water broke in the middle of my Tupperware show, at least we had a big bowl available! Now there's a story...I was born in a Tupperware bowl!*

CHAPTER 26

The Business Side of Dee

Another whole side of my business outside of the character I play is the business of Tupperware—how I book the parties, how I sell my product, how I party-plan with my hostesses for successful parties. And now Tupperware has me come to regional meetings and train people how to sell the product, not to be a drag queen, because even if I took away the character of Dee W. Ieye and tried to sell you Tupperware, it's the importance of what the product does, how it's used, its benefits, its features, which makes me a good salesperson. It's not just being in character, it's *me* telling you why this product is so good and why it's better than anything else you can find on the market.

The process usually starts when you attend a party and decide to have a party of your own. We start the whole negotiation, starting with picking a date, discussing what we're going to do and the fact that we want to have at least twenty-five to thirty-five people at your party, because if I'm coming to your house as a character and I'm doing more than just showing up in my khakis and a tie, I'm putting on a show. I don't want to show up for six people because it's just not worth my time. I've learned over the years that I need to help you have a successful party but at the same time, I want to cover my ass so that I don't drive an hour and a half for six people. So in coaching hostesses, we want to do everything possible to ensure we have a successful party.

What I don't ever know, however, is whether or not we're going to sell anything because you can get thirty people to your house but there's no guarantee that any of those people are going to buy my product. It's a total crap shoot. I have been in situations where I have driven to a neighborhood where I'm in a $2 million house and there are thirty-five people there and my sales are not so good. Or I'll go to a middle-class neighborhood in a not-so-nice house, with people who appear not to have a lot of money, and I sell tons. Even today, it's fascinating to me that I can never second-guess anything. I just never know. I mean, I had a party recently where I just thought it was going to tank, and it was close to a $2000 party.

I was number one in personal retail sales in the nation for four years in a row. My second and third years were just about the time that the economy started to tank, and

I was still selling tons and tons of Tupperware. I think it took about a year for it to really hit people's homes... that's when I started to see that $100 orders became $75 or even $35 orders. And my $40 or $50 orders began disappearing altogether. That was about two years into the recession. And now, I still see it, but it's odd because I'll have people who say, "I really can't spend a lot, here's my $35 order" and then I'll have girls who write checks for $300 without batting an eye. That's a lot of Tupperware! So that's one of those things that I've learned I can never predict with any degree of accuracy, so I don't try.

I actually prefer to go to larger homes because it's easier to accommodate more guests, more room to do my show, and frankly, more space for me to get ready, since it takes me an hour to put on makeup and get dressed. I have been in the most undesirable situations—God bless them—but they were in homes that were not exactly optimum for Dee to get ready! It's me sitting on the floor of a fourteen-year-old kid's bedroom with a little mirror propped up against a drum set and I'm sitting cross-legged in the middle of the floor with a bare light bulb over my head, trying to put my makeup on. Not the best scenario for me.

Over the years I've gotten spoiled, because I've been given the guest suite with the guest bathroom with the fabulous lighting where it's easier for me to put my eyebrows on. Those situations work for me a lot better! But I have to just grin and bear it. I cannot be the arbiter of your home, nor the arbiter of what bathroom I get to use! So I've learned over the years to just roll with the punches!

CHAPTER 27

Are We (Still) Having Fun?

I'm often asked if it's still fun "doing Dee." I can tell you this...when all the planets are lined up correctly and the audience is digging me and the energy in the room is good and I'm sailing through my jokes and I'm sailing through my show, it's like no other feeling. I could have done it 400 times last week and I'm enjoying it in a new and different way as if I've never experienced it before because each show is different. Every good show is different, every mediocre show is different, every bad show is different—for different reasons. I think the thing that's hard for me is all the work I have to do right up to the point of actually walking out on stage and being in front of those women. It's driving to the party, it's dragging my stuff into your house, it's setting up my table, it's putting on the makeup, it's getting dressed, all the stuff that leads up to walking out that door and greeting those people, THAT gets tedious, that falls into the "I can't believe I'm doing this *again*" category. Like when I'm doing it for the fifth night this week.

I have to realize, though, that if it is the fifth night I'm doing it this week, I'm doing very well. It's a job. When I find myself complaining about *oh, I have to get dressed up in drag for this fund raiser, or I have to go now because I have an appearance* or somebody wants me for A,B,C or D, I have to remember that I asked for this. I asked for this job. I created this character, I created her success, I marketed her and brought her to the success she is today. I made my bed and I have to lie in it. It's really no different than people who become Vegas superstars because they wanted to be an actor or a singer, and the universe answered them and gave them exactly what they wanted, and they sit around and bitch that *oh my God, I have to go to the Greek Theater and sing a concert,* and I think yeah, you do because you asked for this and it's your job.

As far as Tupperware goes, I'm a character playing a role, but I have a real affinity for the product. I love this company. I love working for this company. This company has heart and it's really taken care of me. I never thought in a million years that I would be a businessman, ever. I went to school to become an actor. I learned how to stand on stage and project to the back of the house. I didn't go to a business school. I didn't know how to sell anything. And now here I am, having held the title of #1 salesperson four years in a row in the USA and Canada, selling more than anyone else in the company and I am NOT a salesperson!

It's not as if I pulled some things out of my closet and created Dee. Dressing up was not in my experience. As I related earlier, here's how she came about. When I played her at a fund raiser in 2004 I had already created her back story. Just like an actor would approach a script I built her from the ground up. I knew that she was from Tennessee, I knew that she was a ne'er-do-well heir to the Jack Daniels fortune, a beauty pageant contestant who found Tupperware to augment her income. Her costume wasn't really a conscious choice at the beginning, it just seemed appropriately trailer-trashy.

The makeup was a different story. That was designed by a makeup artist friend of mine, Glen Alen Gutierrez. So when I started to do Tupperware, the makeup was a big learning curve for me since I'd never done anything like that before. Glen is fantastic, he is a true master. He taught me how to do Dee's makeup. He taught me by doing one half of my face in front of a mirror and having me do the other half. First he did an eyebrow and then I did an eyebrow, then he did an eyelid and I did an eyelid, and so on. It was so foreign to me that I thought I would never be able to do it,but it has evolved over time. I always feel like I can learn something, do a better job, but the look that Dee W. Ieye has, I would never change that. She's known for the blue eye shadow and pink lips and blond hair. I've tried to change her hair in the past, but it always fails, so

I just stick with what works. I guess if it ain't broke, don't fix it.

The problem is that I get bored and I try to change my clothes or change my hair, anything that will keep it fresh for me. It's fresh for the audiences because they've never seen it before, but now, after all these years, I just like to keep trying things to spice it up for myself. What I've found is that my hair has to match my outrageous makeup because when I've tried other styles that are not as fluffy or bouffant-y or big, there's an imbalance in the overall image. Like Reba McIntire, I just love her, and she always wears the same kind of cute little spiky hairdo, sort of like a little rooster. I once found a blond version of the Reba McIntire hairdo. I bought it in Hollywood because I thought it would be a cute look for Dee, but it DID NOT WORK at all. There has to be volume on the top of my head and volume on the side of my face or it's just a disaster.

Before I left Los Angeles, I took my wig in for a fluff 'n fold and I bought another, in case I wasn't able to find anyone in Ohio who can do the magic that the women in Hollywood can do. But what I learned is that there are drag queens in Columbus, so between them and Facebook, I think I'll be OK!

CHAPTER 28

Keepin' it Real

My colleagues in drag and I have talked often about this whole reality TV thing—and we've all been approached—and it's not necessarily a good thing because it's all based on dirt and drama and getting up into your deep, dark secrets, and because that's not our lives. WE are guys who sell Tupperware as characters and we're really, really successful at what we do. We get booked out months and months in advance and we do press and news programs and they write articles about us. And the truth is, on any given night, most people don't know that Tupperware is still around.

Now I think that there is a show in all of us guys, maybe a scripted sitcom, but it would take the right people to do it and not muck it up. It's hard in Hollywood when you're just a pawn being moved around on a giant plate, but maybe one day it will happen.

I'd like people to know my story because I meet these girls every week who say *this is amazing, tell us how you do what you do.* You know, when this all started, and I had created this character and was approached to sell Tupperware, Geoff thought I'd get the kit in the mail, do one or two parties and then put it away on the shelf to catch dust. Little did I know where this would go—and I shared it recently with a bunch of friends— how would I know when moving to LA in 1996 to be a sitcom star that my life would be what it is today as a guy who dresses up in high heels and tights, lashes and a wig five times a week and doing my own show? It's like going to the theater every night, but in a different place. But that's my life today, selling Tupperware in the suburbs to straight women who love me. It's the best thing that ever happened to me. All I've ever wanted to do was to make people laugh and I get to do that every single night. The first four or five years in this business, that's all I focused on, booking parties and making people laugh. I didn't worry about numbers, didn't worry about what I was making. All that came afterwards. All of that just fell into place. I just wanted to book parties and have fun and make people laugh.

It's important to remember that it's not about the numbers. That last year when I tried to hold onto being number one, after four years of being the nation's top

Tupperware lady, it was so important to me to hold onto that title and I hated my job. I turned my job into not leaving the house to make people laugh but to making sure your party was a $1500 or $2000 party. And if you didn't perform for me, Mrs. Hostess, I was pissed off and I came home miserable and ran myself into the ground, because I turned my business into a numbers game and I took the fun out of it. As soon as I did that, I didn't like what I was doing and I fell out of love with my business. And so the next year was about falling in love with my business again and not worrying about the numbers. My numbers dropped, and a girl in Lancaster, California, became the number one seller that year. I no longer cared about being on top, I had turned it back into wanting to make people laugh and now I'm always in the top five, usually in the top three, and that's just fine. Anyway, Aunt Barbara in New York is kicking everybody's butt. He's having $30,000 months and I don't know how he's doing it. He had a $5000 party recently and I don't know how he even processed all those orders all by himself. When I have more than thirty-five people, I always take someone with me, because it's just too much for one person.

Dee W. Ieye has helped me mature. She really helped me become not afraid of myself. When I stand in front of a group of people now, I feel more empowered now as Kevin because all of that experience standing in front of groups of strangers as Dee W. Ieye has now helped Kevin come out of his shell a little bit more. Now I can stand in front of a ballroom full of people and I can train them about Tupperware without feeling like I'm going to explode from fear. It's intimidating! Actors talk about that all the time…even seasoned actors talk about being terrified when they walk onto the set of a movie. I think it was Jane Fonda who once said that if she wasn't terrified, she would be afraid that she was done learning. Actress Eileen Heckart was a friend of our family so I grew up having little lunches with her. I just loved her. But she said the same thing. I always get a little scared because I don't know who I'm working with. I could be working with someone who knows better than I do, or someone who's not easy to work with, because I'm always working with new people, with a different set of circumstances, different egos.

With Dee as my character, I'm in control. I'm the president and CEO of Dee W. Ieye Enterprises, and this business lives and dies with me, with my decisions. Now, I'm always open to suggestions, but ultimately the buck stops here. One time, however, Geoff said I looked really ugly in a particular wig, and that really hurt my feelings. I never wore that wig again.

CHAPTER 29

You Can Go Home Again

So now that I have been back in Ohio for a couple of years, my business is as successful as it was in Los Angeles. It's amazing. And my company is growing with new recruits and people who want to share in the Tupperware Opportunity. Changing lives, making dreams come true.

I wanted a big house to share with Geoff. I wanted to be around family and friends to share our wonderful life. And I have achieved that dream. For years, I thought it might be in Hollywood, in some grand McMansion, surrounded by celebrities and Hollywood players. Nope. It's in Ohio.

Loving life, enjoying my family, friends and Tupperware Team.

You never know what the Universe is going to have in store for you. But I kept believing, kept dreaming and kept a positive attitude, sometimes even in the not-so-perfect situations.

When I left Ohio for that *Frasier* episode and newfound fame in Hollywood, I said I'd never return to "Podunk" Columbus, Ohio. Well, never say never. I am back. And having explored what I thought to be greener pastures— well, Dorothy—I can assure you, *there's no place like home!*

CPSIA information can be obtained
at www.ICGtesting.com
Printed in the USA
FFOW03n1804231014
8287FF